FAITHFUL LOVE

LOVEGODGREATLY.COM

FAITHFUL LOVE

Published in Dallas by Love God Greatly.

Special thanks to:
Photos from: unsplash.com
Recipes from: adihadean.ro

Printed in the United States of America

Library of Congress Cataloging-in-Publication Data

Printed in the United States of America

24 23 22 21 20 19

6 5 4 3 2 1

AT LOVE GOD GREATLY, YOU'LL FIND REAL, AUTHENTIC WOMEN. WOMEN WHO ARE IMPERFECT, YET FORGIVEN.

Women who desire less of us, and a whole lot more of Jesus. Women who long to know God through His Word, because we know that Truth transforms and sets us free. Women who are better together, saturated in God's Word and in community with one another.

Welcome, friend. We're so glad you're here...

QUARTERS ONLY
50¢
TO OPERATE TURN HANDLE ONE FULL TURN
50¢

CONTENTS

WELCOME

We are glad you have decided to join us in this Bible study! First of all, please know that you have been prayed for! It is not a coincidence you are participating in this study.

Our prayer for you is simple: that you will grow closer to our Lord as you dig into His Word each and every day! As you develop the discipline of being in God's Word on a daily basis, our prayer is that you will fall in love with Him even more as you spend time reading from the Bible.

Each day before you read the assigned Scripture(s), pray and ask God to help you understand it. Invite Him to speak to you through His Word. Then listen. It's His job to speak to you, and it's your job to listen and obey.

Take time to read the verses over and over again. We are told in Proverbs to search and you will find: "Search for it like silver, and hunt for it like hidden treasure. Then you will understand" (Prov. 2:4–5 NCV).

All of us here at Love God Greatly can't wait for you to get started, and we hope to see you at the finish line. Endure, persevere, press on—and don't give up! Finish well what you are beginning today. We will be here every step of the way, cheering you on! We are in this together. Fight to rise early, to push back the stress of the day, to sit alone and spend time in God's Word! Let's see what God has in store for you in this study! Journey with us as we learn to love God greatly with our lives!

As you go through this study, join us in the following resources below:

- Weekly Blog Posts
- Weekly Memory Verses
- Weekly Challenges
- Facebook, Twitter, Instagram
- LoveGodGreatly.com
- Hashtags: #LoveGodGreatly

RESOURCES

Join Us

ONLINE

lovegodgreatly.com

STORE

lovegodgreatly.com/store

FACEBOOK

facebook.com/LoveGodGreatly

INSTAGRAM

instagram.com/lovegodgreatlyofficial

TWITTER

@_LoveGodGreatly

DOWNLOAD THE APP

CONTACT US

info@lovegodgreatly.com

CONNECT

#LoveGodGreatly

LOVE GOD GREATLY

Love God Greatly (LGG) is a beautiful community of women who use a variety of technology platforms to keep each other accountable in God's Word. We start with a simple Bible reading plan, but it doesn't stop there.

Some women gather in homes and churches locally, while others connect online with women across the globe. Whatever the method, we lovingly lock arms and unite for this purpose: to love God greatly with our lives.

Would you consider reaching out and doing this study with someone?

In today's fast-paced technology-driven world, it would be easy to study God's Word in an isolated environment that lacks encouragement or support, but that isn't the intention here at Love God Greatly. God created us to live in community with Him and with those around us.

We need each other, and we live life better together. Because of this, would you consider reaching out and doing this study with someone?

Rest assured we'll be studying right alongside you—learning with you, cheering for you, enjoying sweet fellowship, and smiling from ear to ear as we watch God unite women together—intentionally connecting hearts and minds for His glory.

So here's the challenge: call your mom, your sister, your grandma, the girl across the street, or the college friend across the country. Gather a group of girls from your church or workplace, or meet in a coffee shop with friends you have always wished you knew better.

Arm-in-arm and hand-in-hand, let's do this thing...together.

SOAP STUDY

HOW AND WHY TO SOAP

In this study we offer you a study journal to accompany the verses we are reading. This journal is designed to help you interact with God's Word and learn to dig deeper, encouraging you to slow down and reflect on what God is saying to you that day.

At Love God Greatly, we use the SOAP Bible study method. Before beginning, let's take a moment to define this method and share why we recommend using it during your quiet time in the following pages.

The most important ingredients in the SOAP method are your interaction with God's Word and your application of His Word to your life.

It's one thing to simply read Scripture. But when you interact with it, intentionally slowing down to really reflect on it, suddenly words start popping off the page. The SOAP method allows you to dig deeper into Scripture and see more than you would if you simply read the verses and then went on your merry way.

The most important ingredients in the SOAP method are your interaction with God's Word and your application of His Word to your life:

Blessed is the one who does not walk in step with the wicked or stand in the way that sinners take or sit in the company of mockers, but whose delight is in the law of the LORD, and who meditates on his law day and night. That person is like a tree planted by streams of water, which yields its fruit in season and whose leaf does not wither—whatever they do prospers.
(Ps. 1:1–3, NIV)

Please take the time to SOAP through our Bible studies and see for yourself how much more you get from your daily reading.

You'll be amazed.

SOAP STUDY *(CONTINUED)*

WHAT DOES SOAP MEAN?

MONDAY

READ
Colossians 1:5–8

SOAP
Colossians 1:5–8

Scripture

WRITE OUT THE SCRIPTURE PASSAGE FOR THE DAY.

The faith and love that spring from the hope stored up for you in heaven and about which you have already heard in the true message of the gospel that has come to you. In the same way, the gospel is bearing fruit and growing throughout the whole world just as it has been doing among you since the day you heard it and truly understood God's grace. You learned it from Epaphras, our dear fellow servant, who is a faithful minister of Christ on our behalf, and who also told us of your love in the Spirit.

Observations

WRITE DOWN 1 OR 2 OBSERVATIONS FROM THE PASSAGE.

When you combine faith and love, you get hope. We must remember that our hope is in heaven; it is yet to come. The gospel is the Word of truth. The gospel is continually bearing fruit and growing from the first day to the last. It just takes one person to change a whole community Epaphras.

S STANDS FOR **SCRIPTURE**

Physically write out the verses.

You'll be amazed at what God will reveal to you just by taking the time to slow down and write out what you are reading!

O STANDS FOR **OBSERVATION**

What do you see in the verses that you're reading?

Who is the intended audience? Is there a repetition of words?

What words stand out to you?

A STANDS FOR **APPLICATION**

This is when God's Word becomes personal.

What is God saying to you today?

How can you apply what you just read to your own personal life?

What changes do you need to make? Is there action you need to take?

Applications

WRITE DOWN 1 OR 2 APPLICATIONS FROM THE PASSAGE.

God used one man, Epaphras, to change a whole town. I was reminded that we are simply called to tell others about Christ; it's God's job to spread the gospel, to grow it, and have it bear fruit. I felt today's verses were almost directly spoken to Love God Greatly women: The gospel is bearing fruit and growing throughout the whole world just as it has been doing among you since the day you heard it and truly understood God's grace.

Pray

WRITE OUT A PRAYER OVER WHAT YOU LEARNED FROM TODAY'S PASSAGE.

Dear Lord, please help me to be an Epaphras, to tell others about You and then leave the results in Your loving hands. Please help me to understand and apply personally what I have read today to my life, thereby becoming more and more like You each and every day. Help me to live a life that bears the fruit of faith and love, anchoring my hope in heaven, not here on earth. Help me to remember that the best is yet to come!

P STANDS FOR **PRAYER**

Pray God's Word back to Him. Spend time thanking Him.

If He has revealed something to you during this time in His Word, pray about it.

If He has revealed some sin that is in your life, confess. And remember, He loves you dearly.

A RECIPE FOR YOU

PAPANAŞI

Makes 11 servings

Ingredients

450 grams (16 oz) of sweet cheese (ricotta cheese may be used)

100 grams (1/2 cup) sugar

2 eggs

the zest from one lemon

1 tsp vanilla extract

300 grams (1.5 cups) flour

5 grams (1 tsp) baking powder

For the topping you will need sour cream and jam, or you can make fresh jam (in a small sauce pan, heat 400 grams (2 cups) frozen fruits with 150 grams (3/4 cup) sugar and 100 ml (1/4 cup) water until you have the consistency you like).

Directions

- Combine the cheese, sugar, eggs, lemon zest and vanilla in a bowl and mix with a fork. Add the flour and baking powder and knead the dough with your hands until all the flour is incorporated in the mixture.
- Make 11 large balls and 11 small balls from the dough. In the middle of the big ones form a hole with your finger (like a donut).
- In a sauce pan pour 2-3 fingers of oil and heat it for a couple of minutes on low heat. Fry the dough balls until they are golden brown.
- Place on a paper towel to cool off and drain any excess oil for a few minutes.
- Add one tablespoon of sour cream and one teaspoon of jam on the bigger donut than add the little one on top of it.
- Enjoy!! Poftă bună!

LGG ROMANIAN TESTIMONY

DIANA GHERASIMIUC, LGG ROMANIA

I first saw "Love God Greatly" on Facebook and I really enjoyed the idea of an online community that would give me the opportunity to study the Bible and meet sisters from all over the world. I joined a group led by a woman in South Africa and it was a really nice experience. I needed a study that would give me a starting point in my daily Bible reading, not something that made me feel like I need to brush up on my theology. I was thrilled by the articles and the fact that those who share their experiences on the blog have the courage to make themselves vulnerable. Too often, I feel like I cannot measure up, and too often I see sisters – and others see me – as competition. LGG helped me understand once again that Christ is not just my only hope but all I need to define my identity.

Christ is not just my only hope but all I need to define my identity.

I enjoyed the studies so much that I recommended them to my friends, and I was thrilled to see one of them take on the responsibility to translate the studies and make them available to those who do not speak English. I will continue to pray for this ministry and join in as many studies as I can.

To connect with LGG Romanian Branch:

- lovegodgreatly.com/romanian
- facebook.com/ILoveGodGreatlyRomania
- facebook.com/groups/308374519671962

Do you know someone who could use our *Love God Greatly* Bible studies in Romanian? If so, make sure and tell them about LGG Romanian and all the amazing Bible study resources we provide to help equip them with God's Word!!!

FAITHFUL LOVE

Let's Begin

INTRODUCTION

FAITHFUL LOVE

They had not remained faithful to God, but He remained faithful to them.

The book of Hosea was written to show the people of Israel the faithful love of God, His *hesed*. Israel had rebelled against God over and over again. The kings of Israel had led the people astray, followed false gods, and defiled the temple of God. The people had forgotten who they were and Whose they were. Israel had turned from God, from the One who had chosen them, protected them, provided for them, and blessed them. They had prostituted themselves with other gods and other nations. Their adulterous and idolatrous hearts had taken them far from God.

Hosea was just a man.

He was a prophet in Israel with a unique calling from God. He was asked to marry a prostitute and remain faithful and loyal to her. Hosea married Gomer, who was unfaithful to him. Yet over and over, Hosea redeems Gomer and brings her back to himself.

God gave Hosea a specific calling and a specific message for the people of Israel. Hosea's faithful love to Gomer was meant to display the faithful love of God for Israel.

The book of Hosea is prophecy, with prose and narrative that is often challenging and confusing. As we study this incredible story, our prayer is that we may gain a fresh perspective of God's character. Even in the harsh words of prophecy, we can see God's *hesed*, His faithful, covenant-keeping love pursuing the hearts of His people.

God's love is on display throughout the pages of this beautiful story of redemption. His faithful love is still at work, redeeming our stories and bringing us back to Him.

Maybe you'll identify most with Gomer, the unfaithful wife who ran long and hard from Hosea, despite his efforts to win her love. Maybe you'll see yourself in Hosea, discouraged that your efforts seem to fall short no matter what you do. Or maybe you'll identify with the way Hosea is given a hard calling and be encouraged by the way he remains faithful until the end. But above all, you'll see God's faithful love pursue your heart and life over and over again.

As we explore God's great love for us, may we, in turn, learn to love Him greatly with our lives.

READING PLAN

WEEK 1

Monday
READ: Hosea 1:1, 2 Kings 14:23-29
SOAP: Hosea 1:1
For further reading: 2 Chronicles 26-28

Tuesday
READ: Hosea 1:2, 1 Kings 15:33-16:7, 1 Kings 16:23-34
SOAP: 1 Kings 16:26

Wednesday
READ: Hosea 1:3-5, 2 Kings 17:21-23
SOAP: Hosea 1:5
For further reading: 2 Kings 17:7-20

Thursday
READ: Hosea 1:6-7, 2 Chronicles 29:1-2, 2 Chronicles 32:20-23
SOAP: Hosea 1:7
For further reading: 2 Chronicles 29-32

Friday
READ: Hosea 1:8-2:1, Ezekiel 37:20-28
SOAP: Hosea 1:10

WEEK 2

Monday
READ: Hosea 2:2-13, Deuteronomy 30:19-20
SOAP: Deuteronomy 30:19-20
For further reading: Deuteronomy 30:11-20

Tuesday
READ: Hosea 2:14-23, Psalm 71:20-21
SOAP: Psalm 71:20-21
For further reading: Deuteronomy 30:1-10

Wednesday
READ: Hosea 3:1-5, Jeremiah 3:6-10
SOAP: Hosea 3:1

Thursday
READ: Hosea 4:1-14, Micah 6:8
SOAP: Hosea 4:12
For further reading: Micah 6

Friday
READ: Hosea 4:15-19, Psalm 47
SOAP: Psalm 47:8

WEEK 3

Monday
READ: Hosea 5:1-15, Philippians 3:18-4:1
SOAP: Hosea 5:15

Tuesday
READ: Hosea 6:1-3, Lamentations 3:22-24, 1 Peter 5:6-7
SOAP: Hosea 6:1-3

Wednesday
READ: Hosea 6:4-11, Galatians 6:14-16
SOAP: Hosea 6:6

Thursday
READ: Hosea 7:1-2, Psalm 9:15-16, Proverbs 5:22
SOAP: Psalm 9:16

Friday
READ: Hosea 7:3-12, Psalm 106:40-45
SOAP: Psalm 106:44-45

WEEK 4

Monday
READ: Hosea 7:13-16, Psalm 78:32-39
SOAP: Psalm 78:38

Tuesday
READ: Hosea 8:1-14, Romans 9:22-24
SOAP: Romans 9:22-23

Wednesday
READ: Hosea 9:1-9, Isaiah 10:1-4
SOAP: Hosea 9:9

Thursday
READ: Hosea 9:10-17, Deuteronomy 28:64-65, Psalm 77:7-9
SOAP: Hosea 9:17
For further reading: Psalm 77

Friday
READ: Hosea 10:1-8, Lamentations 1:8,15,18
SOAP: Lamentations 1:18

WEEK 5

Monday
READ: Hosea 10:9-15. Acts 17:27, James 4:8
SOAP: Hosea 10:12
For further reading: Acts 17:22-31

Tuesday
READ: Hosea 11:1-12, Psalm 145:8-9, Micah 7:18-19
SOAP: Hosea 11:8-9

Wednesday
READ: Hosea 12:1-8, Joel 2:13
SOAP: Hosea 12:5-6
For further reading: Genesis 32:24-32

Thursday
READ: Hosea 12:9-11, Romans 8:38-39
SOAP: Hosea 12:9

Friday
READ: Hosea 12:12-14, 2 Kings 7:7-9, Micah 6:16
SOAP: Hosea 12:14
For further reading: Genesis 29:1-20

WEEK 6

Monday
READ: Hosea 13:1-3, Psalm 1
SOAP: Psalm 1:6

Tuesday
READ: Hosea 13:4-14, Mark 10:45
SOAP: Hosea 13:14
For further reading: John 13:1-17

Wednesday
READ: Hosea 13:15-16, Jeremiah 4:11-12, Jeremiah 51:36
SOAP: Jeremiah 51:36

Thursday
READ: Hosea 14:1-3, Nehemiah 1:9, 2 Peter 3:9
SOAP: Hosea 14:2

Friday
READ: Hosea 14:4-9, 1 Corinthians 1:25, James 3:17
SOAP: Hosea 14:9

YOUR GOALS

We believe it's important to write out goals for this study. Take some time now and write three goals you would like to focus on as you begin to rise each day and dig into God's Word. Make sure and refer back to these goals throughout the next weeks to help you stay focused. You can do it!

1.

2.

3.

Signature:

Date:

WEEK 1

Yet the number of the children of Israel shall be like the sand of the sea, which cannot be measured or numbered. And in the place where it was said to them, "You are not my people," it shall be said to them, "Children of the living God."

HOSEA 1:10

PRAYER

WRITE DOWN YOUR PRAYER REQUESTS
AND PRAISES FOR EACH DAY.

Prayer focus for this week:
Spend time praying for your family members.

MONDAY

TUESDAY

WEDNESDAY

THURSDAY

FRIDAY

CHALLENGE

**You can find this listed in our Monday blog post.*

MONDAY

Scripture for Week 1

Hosea 1:1

1 The word of the Lord that came to Hosea, the son of Beeri, in the days of Uzziah, Jotham, Ahaz, and Hezekiah, kings of Judah, and in the days of Jeroboam the son of Joash, king of Israel.

2 Kings 14:23-29

23 In the fifteenth year of Amaziah the son of Joash, king of Judah, Jeroboam the son of Joash, king of Israel, began to reign in Samaria, and he reigned forty-one years. 24 And he did what was evil in the sight of the Lord. He did not depart from all the sins of Jeroboam the son of Nebat, which he made Israel to sin. 25 He restored the border of Israel from Lebo-hamath as far as the Sea of the Arabah, according to the word of the Lord, the God of Israel, which he spoke by his servant Jonah the son of Amittai, the prophet, who was from Gath-hepher. 26 For the Lord saw that the affliction of Israel was very bitter, for there was none left, bond or free, and there was none to help Israel. 27 But the Lord had not said that he would blot out the name of Israel from under heaven, so he saved them by the hand of Jeroboam the son of Joash.

28 Now the rest of the acts of Jeroboam and all that he did, and his might, how he fought, and how he restored Damascus and Hamath to Judah in Israel, are they not written in the Book of the Chronicles of the Kings of Israel? 29 And Jeroboam slept with his fathers, the kings of Israel, and Zechariah his son reigned in his place.

For further reading: 2 Chronicles 26-28

MONDAY

READ:
Hosea 1:1, 2 Kings 14:23-29

SOAP:
Hosea 1:1

Scripture

WRITE OUT THE SCRIPTURE PASSAGE FOR THE DAY.

Observations

WRITE DOWN 1 OR 2 OBSERVATIONS FROM THE PASSAGE.

Applications

WRITE
DOWN 1 OR 2
APPLICATIONS
FROM THE
PASSAGE.

Pray

WRITE OUT
A PRAYER
OVER WHAT
YOU LEARNED
FROM TODAY'S
PASSAGE.

TUESDAY

Scripture for Week 1

Hosea 1:2

2 When the Lord first spoke through Hosea, the Lord said to Hosea, "Go, take to yourself a wife of whoredom and have children of whoredom, for the land commits great whoredom by forsaking the Lord."

1 Kings 15:33-16:7

33 In the third year of Asa king of Judah, Baasha the son of Ahijah began to reign over all Israel at Tirzah, and he reigned twenty-four years. 34 He did what was evil in the sight of the Lord and walked in the way of Jeroboam and in his sin which he made Israel to sin.

1 And the word of the Lord came to Jehu the son of Hanani against Baasha, saying, 2 "Since I exalted you out of the dust and made you leader over my people Israel, and you have walked in the way of Jeroboam and have made my people Israel to sin, provoking me to anger with their sins, 3 behold, I will utterly sweep away Baasha and his house, and I will make your house like the house of Jeroboam the son of Nebat. 4 Anyone belonging to Baasha who dies in the city the dogs shall eat, and anyone of his who dies in the field the birds of the heavens shall eat."

5 Now the rest of the acts of Baasha and what he did, and his might, are they not written in the Book of the Chronicles of the Kings of Israel? 6 And Baasha slept with his fathers and was buried at Tirzah, and Elah his son reigned in his place.7 Moreover, the word of the Lord came by the prophet Jehu the son of Hanani against Baasha and his house, both because of all the evil that he did in the sight of the Lord, provoking him to anger with the work of his hands, in being like the house of Jeroboam, and also because he destroyed it.

1 Kings 16:23-34

23 In the thirty-first year of Asa king of Judah, Omri began to reign over Israel, and he reigned for twelve years; six years he reigned in Tirzah. 24 He bought the hill of Samaria from Shemer for two talents of silver, and he fortified the hill and called the name of the city that he built Samaria, after the name of Shemer, the owner of the hill.

25 Omri did what was evil in the sight of the Lord, and did more evil than all who were before him. 26 For he walked in all the way of Jeroboam the son of Nebat, and in the sins that he made Israel to sin, provoking the Lord, the God of Israel, to anger by their idols. 27 Now the rest of the acts of Omri that he did, and the might that he showed, are they not written in the Book of the Chronicles of the Kings of Israel? 28 And Omri slept with his fathers and was buried in Samaria, and Ahab his son reigned in his place.

29 In the thirty-eighth year of Asa king of Judah, Ahab the son of Omri began to reign over Israel, and Ahab the son of Omri reigned over Israel in Samaria twenty-two years. 30 And Ahab the son of Omri did evil in the sight of the Lord, more than all who were before him. 31 And as if it had been a light thing for him to walk in the sins of Jeroboam the son of Nebat, he took for his wife Jezebel the daughter of Ethbaal king of the Sidonians, and went and served Baal and worshiped him. 32 He erected an altar for Baal in the house of Baal, which he built in Samaria. 33 And Ahab made an Asherah. Ahab did more to provoke the Lord, the God of Israel, to anger than all the kings of Israel who were before him. 34 In his days Hiel of Bethel built Jericho. He laid its foundation at the cost of Abiram his firstborn, and set up its gates at the cost of his youngest son Segub, according to the word of the Lord, which he spoke by Joshua the son of Nun.

TUESDAY

READ:
Hosea 1:2, 1 Kings 15:33-16:7, 1 Kings 16:23-34

SOAP:
1 Kings 16:26

Scripture

WRITE
OUT THE
SCRIPTURE
PASSAGE
FOR THE
DAY.

Observations

WRITE
DOWN 1 OR 2
OBSERVATIONS
FROM THE
PASSAGE.

Applications

WRITE
DOWN 1 OR 2
APPLICATIONS
FROM THE
PASSAGE.

Pray

WRITE OUT
A PRAYER
OVER WHAT
YOU LEARNED
FROM TODAY'S
PASSAGE.

WEDNESDAY

Scripture for Week 1

Hosea 1:3-5

3 So he went and took Gomer, the daughter of Diblaim, and she conceived and bore him a son.

4 And the Lord said to him, "Call his name Jezreel, for in just a little while I will punish the house of Jehu for the blood of Jezreel, and I will put an end to the kingdom of the house of Israel. 5 And on that day I will break the bow of Israel in the Valley of Jezreel."

2 Kings 17:21-23

21 When he had torn Israel from the house of David, they made Jeroboam the son of Nebat king. And Jeroboam drove Israel from following the Lord and made them commit great sin. 22 The people of Israel walked in all the sins that Jeroboam did. They did not depart from them, 23 until the Lord removed Israel out of his sight, as he had spoken by all his servants the prophets. So Israel was exiled from their own land to Assyria until this day.

For further reading: 2 Kings 17:7-20

WEDNESDAY

READ:
Hosea 1:3-5, 2 Kings 17:21-23

SOAP:
Hosea 1:5

Scripture

WRITE
OUT THE
SCRIPTURE
PASSAGE
FOR THE
DAY.

Observations

WRITE
DOWN 1 OR 2
OBSERVATIONS
FROM THE
PASSAGE.

Applications

WRITE DOWN 1 OR 2 APPLICATIONS FROM THE PASSAGE.

Pray

WRITE OUT A PRAYER OVER WHAT YOU LEARNED FROM TODAY'S PASSAGE.

THURSDAY

Scripture for Week 1

Hosea 1:6-7

6 She conceived again and bore a daughter. And the Lord said to him, "Call her name No Mercy, for I will no more have mercy on the house of Israel, to forgive them at all. 7 But I will have mercy on the house of Judah, and I will save them by the Lord their God. I will not save them by bow or by sword or by war or by horses or by horsemen."

2 Chronicles 29:1-2

1 Hezekiah began to reign when he was twenty-five years old, and he reigned twenty-nine years in Jerusalem. His mother's name was Abijah the daughter of Zechariah. 2 And he did what was right in the eyes of the Lord, according to all that David his father had done.

2 Chronicles 32:20-23

20 Then Hezekiah the king and Isaiah the prophet, the son of Amoz, prayed because of this and cried to heaven. 21 And the Lord sent an angel, who cut off all the mighty warriors and commanders and officers in the camp of the king of Assyria. So he returned with shame of face to his own land. And when he came into the house of his god, some of his own sons struck him down there with the sword. 22 So the Lord saved Hezekiah and the inhabitants of Jerusalem from the hand of Sennacherib king of Assyria and from the hand of all his enemies, and he provided for them on every side. 23 And many brought gifts to the Lord to Jerusalem and precious things to Hezekiah king of Judah, so that he was exalted in the sight of all nations from that time onward.

For further reading: 2 Chronicles 29-32

THURSDAY

READ:
Hosea 1:6-7, 2 Chronicles 29:1-2, 2 Chronicles 32:20-23

SOAP:
Hosea 1:7

Scripture

WRITE OUT THE SCRIPTURE PASSAGE FOR THE DAY.

Observations

WRITE DOWN 1 OR 2 OBSERVATIONS FROM THE PASSAGE.

Applications

WRITE DOWN 1 OR 2 APPLICATIONS FROM THE PASSAGE.

Pray

WRITE OUT A PRAYER OVER WHAT YOU LEARNED FROM TODAY'S PASSAGE.

FRIDAY

Scripture for Week 1

Hosea 1:8-2:1

8 When she had weaned No Mercy, she conceived and bore a son. 9 And the Lord said, "Call his name Not My People, for you are not my people, and I am not your God."

10 Yet the number of the children of Israel shall be like the sand of the sea, which cannot be measured or numbered. And in the place where it was said to them, "You are not my people," it shall be said to them, "Children of the living God."11 And the children of Judah and the children of Israel shall be gathered together, and they shall appoint for themselves one head. And they shall go up from the land, for great shall be the day of Jezreel.

1 Say to your brothers, "You are my people," and to your sisters, "You have received mercy."

Ezekiel 37:20-28

20 When the sticks on which you write are in your hand before their eyes, 21 then say to them, Thus says the Lord God: Behold, I will take the people of Israel from the nations among which they have gone, and will gather them from all around, and bring them to their own land. 22 And I will make them one nation in the land, on the mountains of Israel. And one king shall be king over them all, and they shall be no longer two nations, and no longer divided into two kingdoms. 23 They shall not defile themselves anymore with their idols and their detestable things, or with any of their transgressions. But I will save them from all the backslidings in which they have sinned, and will cleanse them; and they shall be my people, and I will be their God.

24 "My servant David shall be king over them, and they shall all have one shepherd. They shall walk in my rules and be careful to obey my statutes. 25 They shall dwell in the land that I gave to my servant Jacob, where your fathers lived. They and their children and their children's children shall dwell there forever, and David my servant shall be their prince forever. 26 I will make a covenant of peace with them. It shall be an everlasting covenant with them. And I will set them in their land and multiply them, and will set my sanctuary in their midst forevermore.27 My dwelling place shall be with them, and I will be their God, and they shall be my people. 28 Then the nations will know that I am the Lord who sanctifies Israel, when my sanctuary is in their midst forevermore."

FRIDAY

READ:
Hosea 1:8-2:1, Ezekiel 37:20-28

SOAP:
Hosea 1:10

Scripture

WRITE
OUT THE
SCRIPTURE
PASSAGE
FOR THE
DAY.

Observations

WRITE
DOWN 1 OR 2
OBSERVATIONS
FROM THE
PASSAGE.

Applications

WRITE DOWN 1 OR 2 APPLICATIONS FROM THE PASSAGE.

Pray

WRITE OUT A PRAYER OVER WHAT YOU LEARNED FROM TODAY'S PASSAGE.

REFLECTION QUESTIONS

1. What command does God give the prophet Hosea? What was strange or out of the ordinary about this command?

2. How do you typically respond when God asks you to do something challenging, difficult, or unprecedented?

3. How did God respond to Israel's sin? Did God give Israel opportunities to repent?

4. What promises does God make at the end of Hosea 1?

5. What do these promises tell us about the heart of God?

NOTES

WEEK 2

God reigns over the nations;
God sits on his holy throne.

PSALM 47:8

PRAYER

WRITE DOWN YOUR PRAYER REQUESTS AND PRAISES FOR EACH DAY.

Prayer focus for this week:
Spend time praying for your country.

MONDAY

TUESDAY

WEDNESDAY

THURSDAY

FRIDAY

CHALLENGE

**You can find this listed in our Monday blog post.*

MONDAY

Scripture for Week 2

Hosea 2:2-13

2 "Plead with your mother, plead—
for she is not my wife,
and I am not her husband—
that she put away her whoring from her face,
and her adultery from between her breasts;
3 lest I strip her naked
and make her as in the day she was born,
and make her like a wilderness,
and make her like a parched land,
and kill her with thirst.
4 Upon her children also I will have no mercy,
because they are children of whoredom.
5 For their mother has played the whore;
she who conceived them has acted shamefully.
For she said, 'I will go after my lovers,
who give me my bread and my water,
my wool and my flax, my oil and my drink.'
6 Therefore I will hedge up her way with thorns,
and I will build a wall against her,
so that she cannot find her paths.
7 She shall pursue her lovers
but not overtake them,
and she shall seek them
but shall not find them.
Then she shall say,
'I will go and return to my first husband,
for it was better for me then than now.'
8 And she did not know
that it was I who gave her
the grain, the wine, and the oil,
and who lavished on her silver and gold,
which they used for Baal.
9 Therefore I will take back
my grain in its time,
and my wine in its season,
and I will take away my wool and my flax,
which were to cover her nakedness.
10 Now I will uncover her lewdness
in the sight of her lovers,
and no one shall rescue her out of my hand.
11 And I will put an end to all her mirth,
her feasts, her new moons, her Sabbaths,
and all her appointed feasts.
12 And I will lay waste her vines and her fig trees,
of which she said,
'These are my wages,
which my lovers have given me.'
I will make them a forest,
and the beasts of the field shall devour them.
13 And I will punish her for the feast days of the Baals
when she burned offerings to them
and adorned herself with her ring and jewelry,
and went after her lovers
and forgot me, declares the Lord.

Deuteronomy 30:19-20

19 I call heaven and earth to witness against you today, that I have set before you life and death, blessing and curse. Therefore choose life, that you and your offspring may live, 20 loving the Lord your God, obeying his voice and holding fast to him, for he is your life and length of days, that you may dwell in the land that the Lord swore to your fathers, to Abraham, to Isaac, and to Jacob, to give them."

For further reading: Deuteronomy 30:11-20

MONDAY

READ:
Hosea 2:2-13, Deuteronomy 30:19-20

SOAP:
Deuteronomy 30:19-20

Scripture

WRITE
OUT THE
SCRIPTURE
PASSAGE
FOR THE
DAY.

Observations

WRITE
DOWN 1 OR 2
OBSERVATIONS
FROM THE
PASSAGE.

Applications

WRITE
DOWN 1 OR 2
APPLICATIONS
FROM THE
PASSAGE.

Pray

WRITE OUT
A PRAYER
OVER WHAT
YOU LEARNED
FROM TODAY'S
PASSAGE.

TUESDAY

Scripture for Week 2

Hosea 2:14-23

14 "Therefore, behold, I will allure her,
and bring her into the wilderness,
and speak tenderly to her.
15 And there I will give her her vineyards
and make the Valley of Achor a door of hope.
And there she shall answer as in the days of her youth,
as at the time when she came out of the land of Egypt.

16 "And in that day, declares the Lord, you will call me 'My Husband,' and no longer will you call me 'My Baal.' 17 For I will remove the names of the Baals from her mouth, and they shall be remembered by name no more. 18 And I will make for them a covenant on that day with the beasts of the field, the birds of the heavens, and the creeping things of the ground. And I will abolish the bow, the sword, and war from the land, and I will make you lie down in safety. 19 And I will betroth you to me forever. I will betroth you to me in righteousness and in justice, in steadfast love and in mercy. 20 I will betroth you to me in faithfulness. And you shall know the Lord.

21 "And in that day I will answer, declares the Lord,
I will answer the heavens,
and they shall answer the earth,
22 and the earth shall answer the grain, the wine, and the oil,
and they shall answer Jezreel,
23 and I will sow her for myself in the land.
And I will have mercy on No Mercy,
and I will say to Not My People, 'You are my people';
and he shall say, 'You are my God.'"

Psalm 71:20-21

20 You who have made me see many troubles and calamities
will revive me again;
from the depths of the earth
you will bring me up again.
21 You will increase my greatness
and comfort me again.

For further reading: Deuteronomy 30:1-10

TUESDAY

READ:
Hosea 2:14-23, Psalm 71:20-21

SOAP:
Psalm 71:20-21

Scripture

WRITE
OUT THE
SCRIPTURE
PASSAGE
FOR THE
DAY.

Observations

WRITE
DOWN 1 OR 2
OBSERVATIONS
FROM THE
PASSAGE.

Applications

WRITE DOWN 1 OR 2 APPLICATIONS FROM THE PASSAGE.

Pray

WRITE OUT A PRAYER OVER WHAT YOU LEARNED FROM TODAY'S PASSAGE.

WEDNESDAY

Scripture for Week 2

Hosea 3:1-5

1 And the Lord said to me, "Go again, love a woman who is loved by another man and is an adulteress, even as the Lord loves the children of Israel, though they turn to other gods and love cakes of raisins." 2 So I bought her for fifteen shekels of silver and a homer and a lethech of barley. 3 And I said to her, "You must dwell as mine for many days. You shall not play the whore, or belong to another man; so will I also be to you." 4 For the children of Israel shall dwell many days without king or prince, without sacrifice or pillar, without ephod or household gods. 5 Afterward the children of Israel shall return and seek the Lord their God, and David their king, and they shall come in fear to the Lord and to his goodness in the latter days.

Jeremiah 3:6-10

6 The Lord said to me in the days of King Josiah: "Have you seen what she did, that faithless one, Israel, how she went up on every high hill and under every green tree, and there played the whore? 7 And I thought, 'After she has done all this she will return to me,' but she did not return, and her treacherous sister Judah saw it.8 She saw that for all the adulteries of that faithless one, Israel, I had sent her away with a decree of divorce. Yet her treacherous sister Judah did not fear, but she too went and played the whore. 9 Because she took her whoredom lightly, she polluted the land, committing adultery with stone and tree. 10 Yet for all this her treacherous sister Judah did not return to me with her whole heart, but in pretense, declares the Lord."

WEDNESDAY

READ:
Hosea 3:1-5, Jeremiah 3:6-10

SOAP:
Hosea 3:1

Scripture

WRITE
OUT THE
SCRIPTURE
PASSAGE
FOR THE
DAY.

Observations

WRITE
DOWN 1 OR 2
OBSERVATIONS
FROM THE
PASSAGE.

Applications

WRITE DOWN 1 OR 2 APPLICATIONS FROM THE PASSAGE.

Pray

WRITE OUT A PRAYER OVER WHAT YOU LEARNED FROM TODAY'S PASSAGE.

THURSDAY

Scripture for Week 2

Hosea 4:1-14

1 Hear the word of the Lord, O children of Israel,
for the Lord has a controversy with the inhabitants of the land.
There is no faithfulness or steadfast love,
and no knowledge of God in the land;
2 there is swearing, lying, murder, stealing, and committing adultery;
they break all bounds, and bloodshed follows bloodshed.
3 Therefore the land mourns,
and all who dwell in it languish,
and also the beasts of the field
and the birds of the heavens,
and even the fish of the sea are taken away.
4 Yet let no one contend,
and let none accuse,
for with you is my contention, O priest.
5 You shall stumble by day;
the prophet also shall stumble with you by night;
and I will destroy your mother.
6 My people are destroyed for lack of knowledge;
because you have rejected knowledge,
I reject you from being a priest to me.
And since you have forgotten the law of your God,
I also will forget your children.
7 The more they increased,
the more they sinned against me;
I will change their glory into shame.
8 They feed on the sin of my people;
they are greedy for their iniquity.
9 And it shall be like people, like priest;
I will punish them for their ways
and repay them for their deeds.
10 They shall eat, but not be satisfied;
they shall play the whore, but not multiply,
because they have forsaken the Lord
to cherish 11 whoredom, wine, and new wine,
which take away the understanding.
12 My people inquire of a piece of wood,
and their walking staff gives them oracles.
For a spirit of whoredom has led them astray,
and they have left their God to play the whore.
13 They sacrifice on the tops of the mountains
and burn offerings on the hills,
under oak, poplar, and terebinth,
because their shade is good.
Therefore your daughters play the whore,
and your brides commit adultery.
14 I will not punish your daughters when they play the whore,
nor your brides when they commit adultery;
for the men themselves go aside with prostitutes
and sacrifice with cult prostitutes,
and a people without understanding shall come to ruin.

Micah 6:8

8 He has told you, O man, what is good;
and what does the Lord require of you
but to do justice, and to love kindness,
and to walk humbly with your God?

For further reading: Micah 6

THURSDAY

READ:
Hosea 4:1-14, Micah 6:8

SOAP:
Hosea 4:12

Scripture

WRITE
OUT THE
SCRIPTURE
PASSAGE
FOR THE
DAY.

Observations

WRITE
DOWN 1 OR 2
OBSERVATIONS
FROM THE
PASSAGE.

Applications

WRITE
DOWN 1 OR 2
APPLICATIONS
FROM THE
PASSAGE.

Pray

WRITE OUT
A PRAYER
OVER WHAT
YOU LEARNED
FROM TODAY'S
PASSAGE.

FRIDAY

Scripture for Week 2

Hosea 4:15-19

15 Though you play the whore, O Israel,
 let not Judah become guilty.
Enter not into Gilgal,
 nor go up to Beth-aven,
 and swear not, "As the Lord lives."
16 Like a stubborn heifer,
 Israel is stubborn;
can the Lord now feed them
 like a lamb in a broad pasture?
17 Ephraim is joined to idols;
 leave him alone.
18 When their drink is gone, they give themselves to whoring;
 their rulers dearly love shame.
19 A wind has wrapped them in its wings,
 and they shall be ashamed because of their sacrifices.

Psalm 47

1 Clap your hands, all peoples!
 Shout to God with loud songs of joy!
2 For the Lord, the Most High, is to be feared,
 a great king over all the earth.
3 He subdued peoples under us,
 and nations under our feet.
4 He chose our heritage for us,
 the pride of Jacob whom he loves. Selah
5 God has gone up with a shout,
 the Lord with the sound of a trumpet.
6 Sing praises to God, sing praises!
 Sing praises to our King, sing praises!
7 For God is the King of all the earth;
 sing praises with a psalm!
8 God reigns over the nations;
 God sits on his holy throne.
9 The princes of the peoples gather
 as the people of the God of Abraham.
For the shields of the earth belong to God;
 he is highly exalted!

FRIDAY

READ:
Hosea 4:15-19, Psalm 47

SOAP:
Psalm 47:8

Scripture

WRITE
OUT THE
SCRIPTURE
PASSAGE
FOR THE
DAY.

Observations

WRITE
DOWN 1 OR 2
OBSERVATIONS
FROM THE
PASSAGE.

Applications

WRITE DOWN 1 OR 2 APPLICATIONS FROM THE PASSAGE.

Pray

WRITE OUT A PRAYER OVER WHAT YOU LEARNED FROM TODAY'S PASSAGE.

REFLECTION QUESTIONS

1. Is God justified in the way He rebukes Israel's adultery? Why or why not?

2. Why is it significant that God chooses to forgive Israel again for her adultery? What does this show us about the character of God?

3. What are some of the ways that Israel rejects God? What are the things she turns to instead?

4. What things in your own life cause you to turn away from God or lead your heart into idolatry?

5. Ask God to give you wisdom into what these things are and how you can begin to identify how they may slip into your life.

NOTES

WEEK 3

Let us know; let us press on
to know the Lord;
his going out is sure as the dawn;
he will come to us as the showers,
as the spring rains that
water the earth."

HOSEA 6:3

PRAYER

WRITE DOWN YOUR PRAYER REQUESTS AND PRAISES FOR EACH DAY.

Prayer focus for this week:
Spend time praying for your friends.

MONDAY

TUESDAY

WEDNESDAY

THURSDAY

FRIDAY

CHALLENGE

**You can find this listed in our Monday blog post.*

MONDAY

Scripture for Week 3

Hosea 5:1-15

1 Hear this, O priests!
Pay attention, O house of Israel!
Give ear, O house of the king!
For the judgment is for you;
for you have been a snare at Mizpah
and a net spread upon Tabor.
2 And the revolters have gone deep into slaughter,
but I will discipline all of them.
3 I know Ephraim,
and Israel is not hidden from me;
for now, O Ephraim, you have played the whore;
Israel is defiled.
4 Their deeds do not permit them
to return to their God.
For the spirit of whoredom is within them,
and they know not the Lord.
5 The pride of Israel testifies to his face;
Israel and Ephraim shall stumble in his guilt;
Judah also shall stumble with them.
6 With their flocks and herds they shall go
to seek the Lord,
but they will not find him;
he has withdrawn from them.
7 They have dealt faithlessly with the Lord;
for they have borne alien children.
Now the new moon shall devour them with their fields.
8 Blow the horn in Gibeah,
the trumpet in Ramah.
Sound the alarm at Beth-aven;
we follow you, O Benjamin!
9 Ephraim shall become a desolation
in the day of punishment;
among the tribes of Israel
I make known what is sure.
10 The princes of Judah have become
like those who move the landmark;
upon them I will pour out
my wrath like water.
11 Ephraim is oppressed, crushed in judgment,
because he was determined to go after filth.
12 But I am like a moth to Ephraim,
and like dry rot to the house of Judah.
13 When Ephraim saw his sickness,
and Judah his wound,
then Ephraim went to Assyria,
and sent to the great king.
But he is not able to cure you
or heal your wound.
14 For I will be like a lion to Ephraim,
and like a young lion to the house of Judah.
I, even I, will tear and go away;
I will carry off, and no one shall rescue.
15 I will return again to my place,
until they acknowledge their guilt and seek my face,
and in their distress earnestly seek me.

Philippians 3:18-4:1

18 For many, of whom I have often told you and now tell you even with tears, walk as enemies of the cross of Christ. 19 Their end is destruction, their god is their belly, and they glory in their shame, with minds set on earthly things. 20 But our citizenship is in heaven, and from it we await a Savior, the Lord Jesus Christ,21 who will transform our lowly body to be like his glorious body, by the power that enables him even to subject all things to himself.

1 Therefore, my brothers, whom I love and long for, my joy and crown, stand firm thus in the Lord, my beloved.

MONDAY

READ:
Hosea 5:1-15, Philippians 3:18-4:1

SOAP:
Hosea 5:15

Scripture

WRITE
OUT THE
SCRIPTURE
PASSAGE
FOR THE
DAY.

Observations

WRITE
DOWN 1 OR 2
OBSERVATIONS
FROM THE
PASSAGE.

Applications

WRITE DOWN 1 OR 2 APPLICATIONS FROM THE PASSAGE.

Pray

WRITE OUT A PRAYER OVER WHAT YOU LEARNED FROM TODAY'S PASSAGE.

TUESDAY

Scripture for Week 3

Hosea 6:1-3

1"Come, let us return to the Lord;
for he has torn us, that he may heal us;
he has struck us down, and he will bind us up.
2 After two days he will revive us;
on the third day he will raise us up,
that we may live before him.
3 Let us know; let us press on to know the Lord;
his going out is sure as the dawn;
he will come to us as the showers,
as the spring rains that water the earth."

Lamentations 3:22-24

22 The steadfast love of the Lord never ceases;
his mercies never come to an end;
23 they are new every morning;
great is your faithfulness.
24 "The Lord is my portion," says my soul,
"therefore I will hope in him."

1 Peter 5:6-7

6 Humble yourselves, therefore, under the mighty hand of God so that at the proper time he may exalt you, 7 casting all your anxieties on him, because he cares for you.

TUESDAY

READ:
Hosea 6:1-3, Lamentations 3:22-24, 1 Peter 5:6-7

SOAP:
Hosea 6:1-3

Scripture

WRITE
OUT THE
SCRIPTURE
PASSAGE
FOR THE
DAY.

Observations

WRITE
DOWN 1 OR 2
OBSERVATIONS
FROM THE
PASSAGE.

Applications

WRITE DOWN 1 OR 2 APPLICATIONS FROM THE PASSAGE.

Pray

WRITE OUT A PRAYER OVER WHAT YOU LEARNED FROM TODAY'S PASSAGE.

WEDNESDAY

Scripture for Week 3

Hosea 6:4-11

4 What shall I do with you, O Ephraim?
What shall I do with you, O Judah?
Your love is like a morning cloud,
like the dew that goes early away.
5 Therefore I have hewn them by the prophets;
I have slain them by the words of my mouth,
and my judgment goes forth as the light.
6 For I desire steadfast love and not sacrifice,
the knowledge of God rather than burnt offerings.
7 But like Adam they transgressed the covenant;
there they dealt faithlessly with me.
8 Gilead is a city of evildoers,
tracked with blood.
9 As robbers lie in wait for a man,
so the priests band together;
they murder on the way to Shechem;
they commit villainy.
10 In the house of Israel I have seen a horrible thing;
Ephraim's whoredom is there; Israel is defiled.
11 For you also, O Judah, a harvest is appointed.
When I restore the fortunes of my people,

Galatians 6:14-16

14 But far be it from me to boast except in the cross of our Lord Jesus Christ, by which the world has been crucified to me, and I to the world. 15 For neither circumcision counts for anything, nor uncircumcision, but a new creation. 16 And as for all who walk by this rule, peace and mercy be upon them, and upon the Israel of God.

WEDNESDAY

READ:
Hosea 6:4-11, Galatians 6:14-16

SOAP:
Hosea 6:6

Scripture

WRITE OUT THE SCRIPTURE PASSAGE FOR THE DAY.

Observations

WRITE DOWN 1 OR 2 OBSERVATIONS FROM THE PASSAGE.

Applications

WRITE
DOWN 1 OR 2
APPLICATIONS
FROM THE
PASSAGE.

Pray

WRITE OUT
A PRAYER
OVER WHAT
YOU LEARNED
FROM TODAY'S
PASSAGE.

THURSDAY

Scripture for Week 3

Hosea 7:1-2

1 when I would heal Israel,
the iniquity of Ephraim is revealed,
and the evil deeds of Samaria,
for they deal falsely;
the thief breaks in,
and the bandits raid outside.
2 But they do not consider
that I remember all their evil.
Now their deeds surround them;
they are before my face.

Psalm 9:15-16

15 The nations have sunk in the pit that they made;
in the net that they hid, their own foot has been caught.
16 The Lord has made himself known; he has executed judgment;
the wicked are snared in the work of their own hands. Higgaion. Selah

Proverbs 5:22

22 The iniquities of the wicked ensnare him,
and he is held fast in the cords of his sin.

THURSDAY

READ:
Hosea 7:1-2, Psalm 9:15-16, Proverbs 5:22

SOAP:
Psalm 9:16

Scripture

WRITE
OUT THE
SCRIPTURE
PASSAGE
FOR THE
DAY.

Observations

WRITE
DOWN 1 OR 2
OBSERVATIONS
FROM THE
PASSAGE.

Applications

WRITE DOWN 1 OR 2 APPLICATIONS FROM THE PASSAGE.

Pray

WRITE OUT A PRAYER OVER WHAT YOU LEARNED FROM TODAY'S PASSAGE.

FRIDAY

Scripture for Week 3

Hosea 7:3-12

3 By their evil they make the king glad,
and the princes by their treachery.
4 They are all adulterers;
they are like a heated oven
whose baker ceases to stir the fire,
from the kneading of the dough
until it is leavened.
5 On the day of our king, the princes
became sick with the heat of wine;
he stretched out his hand with mockers.
6 For with hearts like an oven they approach their intrigue;
all night their anger smolders;
in the morning it blazes like a flaming fire.
7 All of them are hot as an oven,
and they devour their rulers.

All their kings have fallen,
and none of them calls upon me.
8 Ephraim mixes himself with the peoples;
Ephraim is a cake not turned.
9 Strangers devour his strength,
and he knows it not;
gray hairs are sprinkled upon him,
and he knows it not.
10 The pride of Israel testifies to his face;
yet they do not return to the Lord their God,
nor seek him, for all this.
11 Ephraim is like a dove,
silly and without sense,
calling to Egypt, going to Assyria.
12 As they go, I will spread over them my net;
I will bring them down like birds of the heavens;
I will discipline them according to the report made to their congregation.

Psalm 106:40-45

40 Then the anger of the Lord was kindled against his people,
and he abhorred his heritage;
41 he gave them into the hand of the nations,
so that those who hated them ruled over them.
42 Their enemies oppressed them,
and they were brought into subjection under their power.
43 Many times he delivered them,
but they were rebellious in
their purposes
and were brought low through their iniquity.
44 Nevertheless, he looked upon their distress,
when he heard their cry.
45 For their sake he remembered his covenant,
and relented according to the abundance of his steadfast love.

FRIDAY

READ:
Hosea 7:3-12, Psalm 106:40-45

SOAP:
Psalm 106:44-45

Scripture

WRITE
OUT THE
SCRIPTURE
PASSAGE
FOR THE
DAY.

Observations

WRITE
DOWN 1 OR 2
OBSERVATIONS
FROM THE
PASSAGE.

Applications

WRITE DOWN 1 OR 2 APPLICATIONS FROM THE PASSAGE.

Pray

WRITE OUT A PRAYER OVER WHAT YOU LEARNED FROM TODAY'S PASSAGE.

REFLECTION QUESTIONS

1. God, in His patience, gives Israel the opportunity to repent. What does this show us about His character?

2. Is God more angered or grieved by Israel's sin?

3. Even though God brings judgment on Israel, what are the people sure He will do for them when they repent?

4. God rebukes Israel because her love had gone to other gods. Why is God's jealousy justified?

5. What does God desire from His people more than sacrifices? How can you align not just your actions toward Him, but your heart as well?

NOTES

WEEK 4

What if God, desiring to show his wrath and to make known his power, has endured with much patience vessels of wrath prepared for destruction, in order to make known the riches of his glory for vessels of mercy, which he has prepared beforehand for glory.

ROMANS 9:22-23

PRAYER

WRITE DOWN YOUR PRAYER REQUESTS AND PRAISES FOR EACH DAY.

Prayer focus for this week:
Spend time praying for your church.

MONDAY

TUESDAY

WEDNESDAY

THURSDAY

FRIDAY

CHALLENGE

**You can find this listed in our Monday blog post.*

MONDAY

Scripture for Week 4

Hosea 7:13-16

13 Woe to them, for they have strayed from me!
Destruction to them, for they have rebelled against me!
I would redeem them,
but they speak lies against me.
14 They do not cry to me from the heart,
but they wail upon their beds;
for grain and wine they gash themselves;
they rebel against me.
15 Although I trained and strengthened their arms,
yet they devise evil against me.
16 They return, but not upward;
they are like a treacherous bow;
their princes shall fall by the sword
because of the insolence of their tongue.
This shall be their derision in the land of Egypt.

Psalm 78:32-39

32 In spite of all this, they still sinned;
despite his wonders, they did not believe.
33 So he made their days vanish like a breath,
and their years in terror.
34 When he killed them, they sought him;
they repented and sought God earnestly.
35 They remembered that God was their rock,
the Most High God their redeemer.
36 But they flattered him with their mouths;
they lied to him with their tongues.
37 Their heart was not steadfast toward him;
they were not faithful to his covenant.
38 Yet he, being compassionate,
atoned for their iniquity
and did not destroy them;
he restrained his anger often
and did not stir up all his wrath.
39 He remembered that they were but flesh,
a wind that passes and comes not again.

MONDAY

READ:
Hosea 7:13-16, Psalm 78:32-39

SOAP:
Psalm 78:38

Scripture

WRITE
OUT THE
SCRIPTURE
PASSAGE
FOR THE
DAY.

Observations

WRITE
DOWN 1 OR 2
OBSERVATIONS
FROM THE
PASSAGE.

Applications

WRITE
DOWN 1 OR 2
APPLICATIONS
FROM THE
PASSAGE.

Pray

WRITE OUT
A PRAYER
OVER WHAT
YOU LEARNED
FROM TODAY'S
PASSAGE.

TUESDAY

Scripture for Week 4

Hosea 8:1-14

1 Set the trumpet to your lips!
One like a vulture is over the house of the Lord,
because they have transgressed my covenant
and rebelled against my law.
2 To me they cry,
"My God, we—Israel—know you."
3 Israel has spurned the good;
the enemy shall pursue him.
4 They made kings, but not through me.
They set up princes, but I knew it not.
With their silver and gold they made idols
for their own destruction.
5 I have spurned your calf, O Samaria.
My anger burns against them.
How long will they be incapable of innocence?
6 For it is from Israel;
a craftsman made it;
it is not God.
The calf of Samaria
shall be broken to pieces.
7 For they sow the wind,
and they shall reap the whirlwind.
The standing grain has no heads;
it shall yield no flour;
if it were to yield,
strangers would devour it.
8 Israel is swallowed up;
already they are among the nations
as a useless vessel.
9 For they have gone up to Assyria,
a wild donkey wandering alone;
Ephraim has hired lovers.
10 Though they hire allies among the nations,
I will soon gather them up.
And the king and princes shall soon writhe
because of the tribute.
11 Because Ephraim has multiplied altars for sinning,
they have become to him altars for sinning.
12 Were I to write for him my laws by the ten thousands,
they would be regarded as a strange thing.
13 As for my sacrificial offerings,
they sacrifice meat and eat it,
but the Lord does not accept them.
Now he will remember their iniquity
and punish their sins;
they shall return to Egypt.
14 For Israel has forgotten his Maker
and built palaces,
and Judah has multiplied fortified cities;
so I will send a fire upon his cities,
and it shall devour her strongholds.

Romans 9:22-24

22 What if God, desiring to show his wrath and to make known his power, has endured with much patience vessels of wrath prepared for destruction, 23 in order to make known the riches of his glory for vessels of mercy, which he has prepared beforehand for glory— 24 even us whom he has called, not from the Jews only but also from the Gentiles?

TUESDAY

READ:
Hosea 8:1-14, Romans 9:22-24

SOAP:
Romans 9:22-23

Scripture

WRITE
OUT THE
SCRIPTURE
PASSAGE
FOR THE
DAY.

Observations

WRITE
DOWN 1 OR 2
OBSERVATIONS
FROM THE
PASSAGE.

Applications

WRITE DOWN 1 OR 2 APPLICATIONS FROM THE PASSAGE.

Pray

WRITE OUT A PRAYER OVER WHAT YOU LEARNED FROM TODAY'S PASSAGE.

WEDNESDAY

Scripture for Week 4

Hosea 9:1-9

1 Rejoice not, O Israel!
Exult not like the peoples;
for you have played the whore, forsaking your God.
You have loved a prostitute's wages
on all threshing floors.
2 Threshing floor and wine vat shall not feed them,
and the new wine shall fail them.
3 They shall not remain in the land of the Lord,
but Ephraim shall return to Egypt,
and they shall eat unclean food in Assyria.
4 They shall not pour drink offerings of wine to the Lord,
and their sacrifices shall not please him.
It shall be like mourners' bread to them;
all who eat of it shall be defiled;
for their bread shall be for their hunger only;
it shall not come to the house of the Lord.
5 What will you do on the day of the appointed festival,
and on the day of the feast of the Lord?
6 For behold, they are going away from destruction;
but Egypt shall gather them;
Memphis shall bury them.
Nettles shall possess their precious things of silver;
thorns shall be in their tents.
7 The days of punishment have come;
the days of recompense have come;
Israel shall know it.
The prophet is a fool;
the man of the spirit is mad,
because of your great iniquity
and great hatred.
8 The prophet is the watchman of Ephraim with my God;
yet a fowler's snare is on all his ways,
and hatred in the house of his God.
9 They have deeply corrupted themselves
as in the days of Gibeah:
he will remember their iniquity;
he will punish their sins.

Isaiah 10:1-4

1 Woe to those who decree iniquitous decrees,
and the writers who keep writing oppression,
2 to turn aside the needy from justice
and to rob the poor of my people of their right,
that widows may be their spoil,
and that they may make the fatherless their prey!
3 What will you do on the day of punishment,
in the ruin that will come from afar?
To whom will you flee for help,
and where will you leave your wealth?
4 Nothing remains but to crouch among the prisoners
or fall among the slain.
For all this his anger has not turned away,
and his hand is stretched out still.

WEDNESDAY

READ:
Hosea 9:1-9, Isaiah 10:1-4

SOAP:
Hosea 9:9

Scripture

WRITE
OUT THE
SCRIPTURE
PASSAGE
FOR THE
DAY.

Observations

WRITE
DOWN 1 OR 2
OBSERVATIONS
FROM THE
PASSAGE.

Applications

WRITE DOWN 1 OR 2 APPLICATIONS FROM THE PASSAGE.

Pray

WRITE OUT A PRAYER OVER WHAT YOU LEARNED FROM TODAY'S PASSAGE.

THURSDAY

Scripture for Week 4

Hosea 9:10-17

10 Like grapes in the wilderness,
I found Israel.
Like the first fruit on the fig tree
in its first season,
I saw your fathers.
But they came to Baal-peor
and consecrated themselves to the thing of shame,
and became detestable like the thing they loved.
11 Ephraim's glory shall fly away like a bird—
no birth, no pregnancy, no conception!
12 Even if they bring up children,
I will bereave them till none is left.
Woe to them
when I depart from them!
13 Ephraim, as I have seen, was like a young palm planted in a meadow;
but Ephraim must lead his children out to slaughter.
14 Give them, O Lord—
what will you give?
Give them a miscarrying womb
and dry breasts.
15 Every evil of theirs is in Gilgal;
there I began to hate them.
Because of the wickedness of their deeds
I will drive them out of my house.
I will love them no more;
all their princes are rebels.
16 Ephraim is stricken;
their root is dried up;
they shall bear no fruit.
Even though they give birth,
I will put their beloved children to death.
17 My God will reject them
because they have not listened to him;
they shall be wanderers among the nations.

Deuteronomy 28:64-65

64 "And the Lord will scatter you among all peoples, from one end of the earth to the other, and there you shall serve other gods of wood and stone, which neither you nor your fathers have known. 65 And among these nations you shall find no respite, and there shall be no resting place for the sole of your foot, but the Lord will give you there a trembling heart and failing eyes and a languishing soul.

Psalm 77:7-9

7 "Will the Lord spurn forever,
and never again be favorable?
8 Has his steadfast love forever ceased?
Are his promises at an end for all time?
9 Has God forgotten to be gracious?
Has he in anger shut up his compassion?" Selah

For further reading: Psalm 77

THURSDAY

READ:
Hosea 9:10-17, Deuteronomy 28:64-65, Psalm 77:7-9

SOAP:
Hosea 9:17

Scripture

WRITE
OUT THE
SCRIPTURE
PASSAGE
FOR THE
DAY.

Observations

WRITE
DOWN 1 OR 2
OBSERVATIONS
FROM THE
PASSAGE.

Applications

WRITE DOWN 1 OR 2 APPLICATIONS FROM THE PASSAGE.

Pray

WRITE OUT A PRAYER OVER WHAT YOU LEARNED FROM TODAY'S PASSAGE.

FRIDAY

Scripture for Week 4

Hosea 10:1-8

10 Israel is a luxuriant vine
that yields its fruit.
The more his fruit increased,
the more altars he built;
as his country improved,
he improved his pillars.
2 Their heart is false;
now they must bear their guilt.
The Lord will break down their altars
and destroy their pillars.
3 For now they will say:
"We have no king,
for we do not fear the Lord;
and a king—what could he do for us?"
4 They utter mere words;
with empty oaths they make covenants;
so judgment springs up like poisonous weeds
in the furrows of the field.
5 The inhabitants of Samaria tremble
for the calf of Beth-aven.
Its people mourn for it, and so do its idolatrous priests—
those who rejoiced over it and over its glory—
for it has departed from them.
6 The thing itself shall be carried to Assyria
as tribute to the great king.
Ephraim shall be put to shame,
and Israel shall be ashamed of his idol.
7 Samaria's king shall perish
like a twig on the face of the waters.
8 The high places of Aven, the sin of Israel,
shall be destroyed.
Thorn and thistle shall grow up
on their altars,
and they shall say to the mountains,
"Cover us,"
and to the hills, "Fall on us."

Lamentations 1:8,15,18

8 Jerusalem sinned grievously;
therefore she became filthy;
all who honored her despise her,
for they have seen her nakedness;
she herself groans
and turns her face away.

15 "The Lord rejected
all my mighty men in my midst;
he summoned an assembly against me
to crush my young men;
the Lord has trodden as in a winepress
the virgin daughter of Judah.

18 "The Lord is in the right,
for I have rebelled against his word;
but hear, all you peoples,
and see my suffering;
my young women and my young men
have gone into captivity.

FRIDAY

READ:
Hosea 10:1-8, Lamentations 1:8,15,18

SOAP:
Lamentations 1:18

Scripture

WRITE
OUT THE
SCRIPTURE
PASSAGE
FOR THE
DAY.

Observations

WRITE
DOWN 1 OR 2
OBSERVATIONS
FROM THE
PASSAGE.

Applications

WRITE DOWN 1 OR 2 APPLICATIONS FROM THE PASSAGE.

Pray

WRITE OUT A PRAYER OVER WHAT YOU LEARNED FROM TODAY'S PASSAGE.

REFLECTION QUESTIONS

1. How does the rebellion of Israel show the righteousness of God?

2. What aspects of God's character are shown through God's responses to Israel's continued disobedience?

3. Why would it be comforting to know that God remembers our sins?

4. How does God turning away from and rejecting His people for a time show His covenant love for them?

5. Does God withhold His compassion?

NOTES

WEEK 5

Sow for yourselves righteousness;
reap steadfast love;
break up your fallow ground,
for it is the time to seek the Lord,
that he may come and
rain righteousness upon you.

HOSEA 10:12

PRAYER

WRITE DOWN YOUR PRAYER REQUESTS AND PRAISES FOR EACH DAY.

Prayer focus for this week:
Spend time praying for missionaries.

MONDAY

TUESDAY

WEDNESDAY

THURSDAY

FRIDAY

CHALLENGE

**You can find this listed in our Monday blog post.*

MONDAY

Scripture for Week 5

Hosea 10:9-15

9 From the days of Gibeah, you have sinned, O Israel;
  there they have continued.
  Shall not the war against the unjust overtake them in Gibeah?
10 When I please, I will discipline them,
  and nations shall be gathered against them
  when they are bound up for their double iniquity.
11 Ephraim was a trained calf
  that loved to thresh,
  and I spared her fair neck;
but I will put Ephraim to the yoke;
  Judah must plow;
  Jacob must harrow for himself.
12 Sow for yourselves righteousness;
  reap steadfast love;
  break up your fallow ground,
for it is the time to seek the Lord,
  that he may come and rain righteousness upon you.
13 You have plowed iniquity;
  you have reaped injustice;
  you have eaten the fruit of lies.
Because you have trusted in your own way
  and in the multitude of your warriors,
14 therefore the tumult of war shall arise among your people,
  and all your fortresses shall be destroyed,
as Shalman destroyed Beth-arbel on the day of battle;
  mothers were dashed in pieces with their children.
15 Thus it shall be done to you, O Bethel,
  because of your great evil.
At dawn the king of Israel
  shall be utterly cut off.

Acts 17:27

27 that they should seek God, and perhaps feel their way toward him and find him. Yet he is actually not far from each one of us,

James 4:8

8 Draw near to God, and he will draw near to you. Cleanse your hands, you sinners, and purify your hearts, you double-minded.

For further reading: Acts 17:22-31

MONDAY

READ:
Hosea 10:9-15, Acts 17:27, James 4:8

SOAP:
Hosea 10:12

Scripture

WRITE
OUT THE
SCRIPTURE
PASSAGE
FOR THE
DAY.

Observations

WRITE
DOWN 1 OR 2
OBSERVATIONS
FROM THE
PASSAGE.

Applications

WRITE DOWN 1 OR 2 APPLICATIONS FROM THE PASSAGE.

Pray

WRITE OUT A PRAYER OVER WHAT YOU LEARNED FROM TODAY'S PASSAGE.

TUESDAY

Scripture for Week 5

Hosea 11:1-12

1 When Israel was a child, I loved him,
and out of Egypt I called my son.
2 The more they were called,
the more they went away;
they kept sacrificing to the Baals
and burning offerings to idols.
3 Yet it was I who taught Ephraim to walk;
I took them up by their arms,
but they did not know that I healed them.
4 I led them with cords of kindness,
with the bands of love,
and I became to them as one who eases the yoke on their jaws,
and I bent down to them and fed them.
5 They shall not return to the land of Egypt,
but Assyria shall be their king,
because they have refused to return to me.
6 The sword shall rage against their cities,
consume the bars of their gates,
and devour them because of their own counsels.
7 My people are bent on turning away from me,
and though they call out to the Most High,
he shall not raise them up at all.
8 How can I give you up, O Ephraim?
How can I hand you over, O Israel?
How can I make you like Admah?
How can I treat you like Zeboiim?
My heart recoils within me;
my compassion grows warm and tender.
9 I will not execute my burning anger;
I will not again destroy Ephraim;
for I am God and not a man,
the Holy One in your midst,
and I will not come in wrath.
10 They shall go after the Lord;
he will roar like a lion;
when he roars,
his children shall come trembling from the west;
11 they shall come trembling like birds from Egypt,
and like doves from the land of Assyria,
and I will return them to their homes,
declares the Lord.
12 Ephraim has surrounded me with lies,
and the house of Israel with deceit,
but Judah still walks with God
and is faithful to the Holy One.

Psalm 145:8-9

8 The Lord is gracious and merciful,
slow to anger and abounding in steadfast love.
9 The Lord is good to all,
and his mercy is over all that he has made.

Micah 7:18-19

18 Who is a God like you, pardoning iniquity
and passing over transgression
for the remnant of his inheritance?
He does not retain his anger forever,
because he delights in steadfast love.
19 He will again have compassion on us;
he will tread our iniquities underfoot.
You will cast all our sins
into the depths of the sea.

TUESDAY

READ:
Hosea 11:1-12, Psalm 145:8-9, Micah 7:18-19

SOAP:
Hosea 11:8-9

Scripture

WRITE
OUT THE
SCRIPTURE
PASSAGE
FOR THE
DAY.

Observations

WRITE
DOWN 1 OR 2
OBSERVATIONS
FROM THE
PASSAGE.

Applications

WRITE DOWN 1 OR 2 APPLICATIONS FROM THE PASSAGE.

Pray

WRITE OUT A PRAYER OVER WHAT YOU LEARNED FROM TODAY'S PASSAGE.

WEDNESDAY

Scripture for Week 5

Hosea 12:1-8

1 Ephraim feeds on the wind
  and pursues the east wind all day long;
they multiply falsehood and violence;
  they make a covenant with Assyria,
  and oil is carried to Egypt.
2 The Lord has an indictment against Judah
  and will punish Jacob according to his ways;
  he will repay him according to his deeds.
3 In the womb he took his brother by the heel,
  and in his manhood he strove with God.
4 He strove with the angel and prevailed;
  he wept and sought his favor.
He met God at Bethel,
  and there God spoke with us—
5 the Lord, the God of hosts,
  the Lord is his memorial name:
6 "So you, by the help of your God, return,
  hold fast to love and justice,
  and wait continually for your God."
7 A merchant, in whose hands are false balances,
  he loves to oppress.
8 Ephraim has said, "Ah, but I am rich;
  I have found wealth for myself;
in all my labors they cannot find in me iniquity or sin."

Joel 2:13

13 and rend your hearts and not your garments."
Return to the Lord your God,
  for he is gracious and merciful,
slow to anger, and abounding in steadfast love;
  and he relents over disaster.

For further reading: Genesis 32:24-32

WEDNESDAY

READ:
Hosea 12:1-8, Joel 2:13

SOAP:
Hosea 12:5-6

Scripture

WRITE
OUT THE
SCRIPTURE
PASSAGE
FOR THE
DAY.

Observations

WRITE
DOWN 1 OR 2
OBSERVATIONS
FROM THE
PASSAGE.

Applications

WRITE DOWN 1 OR 2 APPLICATIONS FROM THE PASSAGE.

Pray

WRITE OUT A PRAYER OVER WHAT YOU LEARNED FROM TODAY'S PASSAGE.

THURSDAY

Scripture for Week 5

Hosea 12:9-11

9 I am the Lord your God
  from the land of Egypt;
I will again make you dwell in tents,
  as in the days of the appointed feast.
10 I spoke to the prophets;
  it was I who multiplied visions,
  and through the prophets gave parables.
11 If there is iniquity in Gilead,
  they shall surely come to nothing:
in Gilgal they sacrifice bulls;
  their altars also are like stone heaps
  on the furrows of the field.

Romans 8:38-39

38 For I am sure that neither death nor life, nor angels nor rulers, nor things present nor things to come, nor powers, 39 nor height nor depth, nor anything else in all creation, will be able to separate us from the love of God in Christ Jesus our Lord.

THURSDAY

READ:
Hosea 12:9-11, Romans 8:38-39

SOAP:
Hosea 12:9

Scripture

WRITE
OUT THE
SCRIPTURE
PASSAGE
FOR THE
DAY.

Observations

WRITE
DOWN 1 OR 2
OBSERVATIONS
FROM THE
PASSAGE.

Applications

WRITE
DOWN 1 OR 2
APPLICATIONS
FROM THE
PASSAGE.

Pray

WRITE OUT
A PRAYER
OVER WHAT
YOU LEARNED
FROM TODAY'S
PASSAGE.

FRIDAY

Scripture for Week 5

Hosea 12:12-14

12 Jacob fled to the land of Aram;
there Israel served for a wife,
and for a wife he guarded sheep.
13 By a prophet the Lord brought Israel up from Egypt,
and by a prophet he was guarded.
14 Ephraim has given bitter provocation;
so his Lord will leave his bloodguilt on him
and will repay him for his disgraceful deeds.

2 Kings 7:7-9

7 So they fled away in the twilight and abandoned their tents, their horses, and their donkeys, leaving the camp as it was, and fled for their lives. 8 And when these lepers came to the edge of the camp, they went into a tent and ate and drank, and they carried off silver and gold and clothing and went and hid them. Then they came back and entered another tent and carried off things from it and went and hid them.

9 Then they said to one another, "We are not doing right. This day is a day of good news. If we are silent and wait until the morning light, punishment will overtake us. Now therefore come; let us go and tell the king's household."

Micah 6:16

16 For you have kept the statutes of Omri,
and all the works of the house of Ahab;
and you have walked in their counsels,
that I may make you a desolation, and your inhabitants a hissing;
so you shall bear the scorn of my people."

For further reading: Genesis 29:1-20

FRIDAY

READ:
Hosea 12:12-14, 2 Kings 7:7-9, Micah 6:16

SOAP:
Hosea 12:14

Scripture

WRITE
OUT THE
SCRIPTURE
PASSAGE
FOR THE
DAY.

Observations

WRITE
DOWN 1 OR 2
OBSERVATIONS
FROM THE
PASSAGE.

Applications

WRITE DOWN 1 OR 2 APPLICATIONS FROM THE PASSAGE.

Pray

WRITE OUT A PRAYER OVER WHAT YOU LEARNED FROM TODAY'S PASSAGE.

REFLECTION QUESTIONS

1. God commands Israel to return to and seek Him. Is God's mercy dependent upon Israel's actions? Is God's mercy toward us dependent upon our actions?

2. Hosea 11:8 says God had a change of heart. Can God change His mind? What are some other examples of God changing His mind?

3. If God can change His mind, does that mean He really knows the future? How does His ability to change His mind contribute to His sovereignty?

4. Is God inconsistent or unpredictable if He can change His mind? How is His willingness to change His mind a comforting thought?

5. How is God's justice affected by His ability to change His mind? How is His mercy affected by the way He changes His mind?

NOTES

WEEK 6

Whoever is wise,
let him understand these things;
whoever is discerning,
let him know them;
for the ways of the Lord are right,
and the upright walk in them,
but transgressors stumble in them.

HOSEA 14:9

PRAYER

WRITE DOWN YOUR PRAYER REQUESTS AND PRAISES FOR EACH DAY.

Prayer focus for this week:
Spend time praying for yourself.

MONDAY

TUESDAY

WEDNESDAY

THURSDAY

FRIDAY

CHALLENGE

**You can find this listed in our Monday blog post.*

MONDAY

Scripture for Week 6

Hosea 13:1-3

1 When Ephraim spoke, there was trembling;
he was exalted in Israel,
but he incurred guilt through Baal and died.
2 And now they sin more and more,
and make for themselves metal images,
idols skillfully made of their silver,
all of them the work of craftsmen.
It is said of them,
"Those who offer human sacrifice kiss calves!"
3 Therefore they shall be like the morning mist
or like the dew that goes early away,
like the chaff that swirls from the threshing floor
or like smoke from a window.

Psalm 1

1 Blessed is the man
who walks not in the counsel of the wicked,
nor stands in the way of sinners,
nor sits in the seat of scoffers;
2 but his delight is in the law of the Lord,
and on his law he meditates day and night.
3 He is like a tree
planted by streams of water
that yields its fruit in its season,
and its leaf does not wither.
In all that he does, he prospers.
4 The wicked are not so,
but are like chaff that the wind drives away.
5 Therefore the wicked will not stand in the judgment,
nor sinners in the congregation of the righteous;
6 for the Lord knows the way of the righteous,
but the way of the wicked will perish.

MONDAY

READ:
Hosea 13:1-3, Psalm 1

SOAP:
Psalm 1:6

Scripture

WRITE
OUT THE
SCRIPTURE
PASSAGE
FOR THE
DAY.

Observations

WRITE
DOWN 1 OR 2
OBSERVATIONS
FROM THE
PASSAGE.

Applications

WRITE DOWN 1 OR 2 APPLICATIONS FROM THE PASSAGE.

Pray

WRITE OUT A PRAYER OVER WHAT YOU LEARNED FROM TODAY'S PASSAGE.

TUESDAY

Scripture for Week 6

Hosea 13:4-14

4 But I am the Lord your God
 from the land of Egypt;
you know no God but me,
 and besides me there is no savior.
5 It was I who knew you in the wilderness,
 in the land of drought;
6 but when they had grazed, they became full,
 they were filled, and their heart was lifted up;
 therefore they forgot me.
7 So I am to them like a lion;
 like a leopard I will lurk beside the way.
8 I will fall upon them like a bear robbed of her cubs;
 I will tear open their breast,
and there I will devour them like a lion,
 as a wild beast would rip them open.
9 He destroys you, O Israel,
 for you are against me, against your helper.
10 Where now is your king, to save you in all your cities?
 Where are all your rulers—
those of whom you said,
 "Give me a king and princes"?
11 I gave you a king in my anger,
 and I took him away in my wrath.
12 The iniquity of Ephraim is bound up;
 his sin is kept in store.
13 The pangs of childbirth come for him,
 but he is an unwise son,
for at the right time he does not present himself
 at the opening of the womb.
14 I shall ransom them from the power of Sheol;
 I shall redeem them from Death.
O Death, where are your plagues?
 O Sheol, where is your sting?
 Compassion is hidden from my eyes.

Mark 10:45

45 For even the Son of Man came not to be served but to serve, and to give his life as a ransom for many."

For further reading: John 13:1-17

TUESDAY

READ:
Hosea 13:4-14, Mark 10:45

SOAP:
Hosea 13:14

Scripture

WRITE
OUT THE
SCRIPTURE
PASSAGE
FOR THE
DAY.

Observations

WRITE
DOWN 1 OR 2
OBSERVATIONS
FROM THE
PASSAGE.

Applications

WRITE DOWN 1 OR 2 APPLICATIONS FROM THE PASSAGE.

Pray

WRITE OUT A PRAYER OVER WHAT YOU LEARNED FROM TODAY'S PASSAGE.

WEDNESDAY

Scripture for Week 6

Hosea 13:15-16

15 Though he may flourish among his brothers,
the east wind, the wind of the Lord, shall come,
rising from the wilderness,
and his fountain shall dry up;
his spring shall be parched;
it shall strip his treasury
of every precious thing.
16 Samaria shall bear her guilt,
because she has rebelled against her God;
they shall fall by the sword;
their little ones shall be dashed in pieces,
and their pregnant women ripped open.

Jeremiah 4:11-12

11 At that time it will be said to this people and to Jerusalem, "A hot wind from the bare heights in the desert toward the daughter of my people, not to winnow or cleanse, 12 a wind too full for this comes for me. Now it is I who speak in judgment upon them."

Jeremiah 51:36

36 Therefore thus says the Lord:
"Behold, I will plead your cause
and take vengeance for you.
I will dry up her sea
and make her fountain dry,

WEDNESDAY

READ:
Hosea 13:15-16, Jeremiah 4:11-12, Jeremiah 51:36

SOAP:
Jeremiah 51:36

Scripture

WRITE
OUT THE
SCRIPTURE
PASSAGE
FOR THE
DAY.

Observations

WRITE
DOWN 1 OR 2
OBSERVATIONS
FROM THE
PASSAGE.

Applications

WRITE
DOWN 1 OR 2
APPLICATIONS
FROM THE
PASSAGE.

Pray

WRITE OUT
A PRAYER
OVER WHAT
YOU LEARNED
FROM TODAY'S
PASSAGE.

THURSDAY

Scripture for Week 6

Hosea 14:1-3

1 Return, O Israel, to the Lord your God,
for you have stumbled because of your iniquity.
2 Take with you words
and return to the Lord;
say to him,
"Take away all iniquity;
accept what is good,
and we will pay with bulls
the vows of our lips.
3 Assyria shall not save us;
we will not ride on horses;
and we will say no more, 'Our God,'
to the work of our hands.
In you the orphan finds mercy."

Nehemiah 1:9

9 but if you return to me and keep my commandments and do them, though your outcasts are in the uttermost parts of heaven, from there I will gather them and bring them to the place that I have chosen, to make my name dwell there.'

2 Peter 3:9

9 The Lord is not slow to fulfill his promise as some count slowness, but is patient toward you, not wishing that any should perish, but that all should reach repentance.

THURSDAY

READ:
Hosea 14:1-3, Nehemiah 1:9, 2 Peter 3:9

SOAP:
Hosea 14:2

Scripture

WRITE OUT THE SCRIPTURE PASSAGE FOR THE DAY.

Observations

WRITE DOWN 1 OR 2 OBSERVATIONS FROM THE PASSAGE.

Applications

WRITE DOWN 1 OR 2 APPLICATIONS FROM THE PASSAGE.

Pray

WRITE OUT A PRAYER OVER WHAT YOU LEARNED FROM TODAY'S PASSAGE.

FRIDAY

Scripture for Week 6

Hosea 14:4-9

4 I will heal their apostasy;
  I will love them freely,
  for my anger has turned from them.
5 I will be like the dew to Israel;
  he shall blossom like the lily;
  he shall take root like the trees of Lebanon;
6 his shoots shall spread out;
  his beauty shall be like the olive,
  and his fragrance like Lebanon.
7 They shall return and dwell beneath my shadow;
  they shall flourish like the grain;
they shall blossom like the vine;
  their fame shall be like the wine of Lebanon.
8 O Ephraim, what have I to do with idols?
  It is I who answer and look after you.
I am like an evergreen cypress;
  from me comes your fruit.
9 Whoever is wise, let him understand these things;
  whoever is discerning, let him know them;
for the ways of the Lord are right,
  and the upright walk in them,
  but transgressors stumble in them.

1 Corinthians 1:25

25 For the foolishness of God is wiser than men, and the weakness of God is stronger than men.

James 3:17

17 But the wisdom from above is first pure, then peaceable, gentle, open to reason, full of mercy and good fruits, impartial and sincere.

FRIDAY

READ:
Hosea 14:4-9, 1 Corinthians 1:25, James 3:17

SOAP:
Hosea 14:9

Scripture

WRITE
OUT THE
SCRIPTURE
PASSAGE
FOR THE
DAY.

Observations

WRITE
DOWN 1 OR 2
OBSERVATIONS
FROM THE
PASSAGE.

Applications

WRITE
DOWN 1 OR 2
APPLICATIONS
FROM THE
PASSAGE.

Pray

WRITE OUT
A PRAYER
OVER WHAT
YOU LEARNED
FROM TODAY'S
PASSAGE.

REFLECTION QUESTIONS

1. How does the book of Hosea show us the wisdom of God? How is God's wisdom different than human wisdom?

2. In what ways does Hosea show us that God's ways are higher than our ways?

3. How does the book of Hosea display God's character? What aspects of God's character are most prominent in the book of Hosea?

4. Hosea shows us the lengths to which God will go to redeem Israel. Does God do the same for us today? How have you seen His hand of redemption in your own life?

5. How does the book of Hosea show you God's faithful love?

NOTES

KNOW THESE TRUTHS

from God's Word

God loves you.

Even when you're feeling unworthy and like the world is stacked against you, God loves you - yes, you - and He has created you for great purpose.

God's Word says, "God so loved the world that He gave His one and only Son, Jesus, that whoever believes in Him shall not perish, but have eternal life" (John 3:16).

Our sin separates us from God.

We are all sinners by nature and by choice, and because of this we are separated from God, who is holy.

God's Word says, "All have sinned and fall short of the glory of God" (Romans 3:23).

Jesus died so that you might have life.

The consequence of sin is death, but your story doesn't have to end there! God's free gift of salvation is available to us because Jesus took the penalty for our sin when He died on the cross.

God's Word says, "For the wages of sin is death, but the free gift of God is eternal life in Christ Jesus our Lord" (Romans 6:23); "God demonstrates His own love toward us, in that while we were yet sinners, Christ died for us" (Romans 5:8).

Jesus lives!

Death could not hold Him, and three days after His body was placed in the tomb Jesus rose again, defeating sin and death forever! He lives today in heaven and is preparing a place in eternity for all who believe in Him.

God's Word says, "In my Father's house are many rooms. If it were not so, would I have told you that I go to prepare a place for you? And if I go and prepare a place for you, I will come again and will take you to myself, that where I am you may be also" (John 14:2-3).

Yes, you can KNOW that you are forgiven.

Accept Jesus as the only way to salvation...

Accepting Jesus as your Savior is not about what you can do, but rather about having faith in what Jesus has already done. It takes recognizing that you are a sinner, believing that Jesus died for your sins, and asking for forgiveness by placing your full trust in Jesus's work on the cross on your behalf.

God's Word says, "If you confess with your mouth that Jesus is Lord and believe in your heart that God raised him from the dead, you will be saved. For with the heart one believes and is justified, and with the mouth one confesses and is saved" (Romans 10:9-10).

Practically, what does that look like?

With a sincere heart, you can pray a simple prayer like this:

God,
I know that I am a sinner.
I don't want to live another day without embracing
the love and forgiveness that You have for me.
I ask for Your forgiveness.
I believe that You died for my sins and rose from the dead.
I surrender all that I am and ask You to be Lord of my life.
Help me to turn from my sin and follow You.
Teach me what it means to walk in freedom as I live under Your grace,
and help me to grow in Your ways as I seek to know You more.
Amen.

If you just prayed this prayer (or something similar in your own words), would you email us at info@lovegodgreatly.com?

We'd love to help get you started on this exciting journey as a child of God!

JOURNEY

WELCOME FRIEND

We're so glad you're here

Love God Greatly exists to inspire, encourage, and equip women all over the world to make God's Word a priority in their lives.

INSPIRE
women to make God's Word a priority in their daily lives through our Bible study resources.

ENCOURAGE
women in their daily walks with God through online community and personal accountability.

EQUIP
women to grow in their faith, so that they can effectively reach others for Christ.

Love God Greatly consists of a beautiful community of women who use a variety of technology platforms to keep each other accountable in God's Word.

We start with a simple Bible reading plan, but it doesn't stop there.

Some gather in homes and churches locally, while others connect online with women across the globe. Whatever the method, we lovingly lock arms and unite for this purpose...to Love God Greatly with our lives.

At Love God Greatly, you'll find real, authentic women. Women who are imperfect, yet forgiven. Women who desire less of us, and a whole lot more of Jesus. Women who long to know God through his Word, because we know that Truth transforms and sets us free. Women who are better together, saturated in God's Word and in community with one another.

Love God Greatly is a 501 (C) (3) non-profit organization. Funding for Love God Greatly comes through donations and proceeds from our online Bible study journals and books. LGG is committed to providing quality Bible study materials and believes finances should never get in the way of a woman being able to participate in one of our studies. All journals and translated journals are available to download for free from LoveGodGreatly.com for those who cannot afford to purchase them. Our journals and books are also available for sale on Amazon. Search for "Love God Greatly" to see all of our Bible study journals and books. 100% of proceeds go directly back into supporting Love God Greatly and helping us inspire, encourage and equip women all over the world with God's Word.

THANK YOU for partnering with us!

WHAT WE OFFER:

18 + Translations | Bible Reading Plans | Online Bible Study
Love God Greatly App | 80 + Countries Served
Bible Study Journals & Books | Community Groups

EACH LGG STUDY INCLUDES:

Three Devotional Corresponding Blog Posts
Memory Verses | Weekly Challenge | Weekly Reading Plan
Reflection Questions And More!

OTHER LOVE GOD GREATLY STUDIES INCLUDE:

Savior | Promises of God | Love the Loveless | Truth Over Lies
1 & 2 Thessalonians | Fear & Anxiety | James | His Name Is...
Philippians | 1 & 2 Timothy | Sold Out | Ruth | Broken & Redeemed
Walking in Wisdom | God With Us | In Everything Give Thanks
You Are Forgiven | David | Ecclesiastes | Growing Through Prayer
Names of God | Galatians | Psalm 119 | 1st & 2nd Peter
Made For Community | The Road To Christmas
The Source Of Gratitude | Esther | You Are Loved

Visit us online at

LOVEGODGREATLY.COM

Made in the USA
Columbia, SC
21 February 2019